No matter where we play, the HEART
These stories are YOUR stories, and
of strong, confident young women

sHe Play

So chase your 'DREAMS', BOTH

OF THE GAME STAYS WITH US <u>FOREVER.</u>
THESE GIRLS ARE THE <u>FUTURE.</u> A GENERATION
LIVING LIFE WITH <u>GUTS AND PASSION.</u>

S WE WIN

ON AND OFF THE FIELD, BECAUSE
WHEN <u>YOU PLAY,</u> WE <u>ALL WIN.</u>

ISBN 13: 978-1-63489-350-3

Library of Congress Catalog Number: 2020907995
Printed in the United States of America
First Printing: 2020

24 23 22 21 20   5 4 3 2 1

Cover and interior design by Mariah Jochai :: Craft-o-Graph

Wise Ink Creative Publishing
807 Broadway St NE
Suite 46
Minneapolis, MN, 55413

To order, visit SHEPLAYSWEWIN.COM.
Reseller discounts available.

She Plays We Win

BY **CHRISTIN ROSE**

This is SHE PLAYS WE WIN, the BOOK!

I hope when you look at these photos, the girls in the book represent a girl or woman you know.
I hope when you look at the determination in their eyes—you see HOPE for the future.
They represent a generation of GIRLS that are proud, strong, and confident.

Some of these girls will become Olympians.
Some will go on to play in college.
Some will coach or play professionally.
Some will break barriers for the first time, some will set records!
Like so many of you out there and the girls you know . . . some will change the world as we know it.

But some, like me, will stop playing.
They will find other passions, and go on to chase new dreams . . . but **they won't ever forget what it feels like to play**.
No. They won't ever forget what it feels like to hit a winning run, or to be in a huddle with all-hands-in.
They won't ever forget the butterflies in their stomach.
They won't ever forget taking a shot a split second before the buzzer sounds.
They won't ever forget the hours, sweat, and effort it took them to get there.
No, none of that ever goes away. It stays in your HEART for the rest of your life.

As this generation grows up and moves on to different arenas, the LOVE of the game will stay with them forever. As the girls you know become women, they will take the grit and hustle from the field, court, race, rink, and so on straight into the game of life and continue to work, practice, improve, show up early, and stay late in EVERYTHING they do.

This is what we applaud in the pages to come and the true meaning of SHE PLAYS WE WIN.

This book is for every girl that understands that notion. And for anyone that has a girl in their life who represents that. It's for you, Dad. It's for you, Coach! It's for you, brother, sister, mom, friend, teacher, aunt, uncle. It's for anyone that knows and BELIEVES in the power of sports for girls.

So, let's celebrate.
Let's honor access to sports for women.
Let's continue to encourage girls to chase their dreams on and off the field.
And let's continue to support girls' athletics because the truth is,
when **SHE PLAYS, WE ALL WIN**.

WSF Women's Sports Foundation

It was so incredibly important to us that **SHE PLAYS WE WIN** pay it forward for all girls and women—now and for future generations.

That is why a portion of our proceeds go to the **Women's Sports Foundation** in support of its mission to enable girls and women to reach their potential in sport and life. WSF exists to unlock the possibilities in every girl and woman through the power of sport, and the images in our book show what limitless potential looks like! We are so incredibly proud to contribute to this amazing nonprofit.

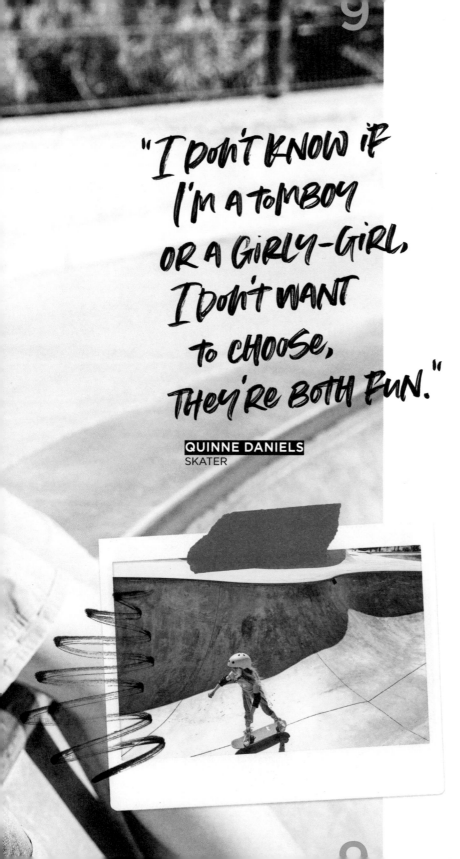

> "I don't know if I'm a tomboy or a girly-girl, I don't want to choose, they're both fun."

QUINNE DANIELS
SKATER

Foreword

FROM THE *FREE PEOPLE* BLOG

Meet the girls of #SHEPLAYSWEWIN, a photo series throwing the spotlight on young girl athletes. Photographer Christin Rose has made it her life quest to foster the self-assurance and strength in young girls that so many of them discover in organized sports. This photography project is her outlet.

Look into the eyes of her portraits, and you see a confidence not only blossoming but radiating from girls who've just uncovered the well of strength their bodies are capable of.

A series about more than just its subjects, it's about any and every young woman who might be moved to action after seeing the images of so many girls like them, who have harnessed this power within themselves.

For girls without the resources and encouragement around them, SHE PLAYS WE WIN proves that if they hear within them a calling to crawl in the dirt, hop on a board, sweat, stink, bleed—do anything duplicitously branded "unladylike" by who-cares-who—then it's all theirs for the taking. That their lives are written not by their gender, not by their society, not by their surrounding media, and not even by fate, but by themselves and themselves alone. Opening a world of possibilities to girls, at an age of self-definition when they need it most.

Look closely, and you can make out a reflection of Christin's younger self. The little girl who once couldn't decide between Barbies and backyard baseball now echoes in the frilly-skirted skater, figuring out if she's a tomboy or girly-girl. Coming full circle, as things so often do.

#SHePlaySWeWIN

SPWV

The amazing thing about this is I started the project to photograph girls who I thought were cool to inspire other girls, but in turn, I ended up

Being the most inspired I've ever been in my entire life — this project changed me FOREVER and it's because of the GIRLS!

—Christin Rose
Photographer

SHE PLAYS WE WIN

HIGHLIGHTS THE TRIALS + TRIUMPHS OF YOUNG FEMALE ATHLETES AGES 7-14. →

AND HAVE

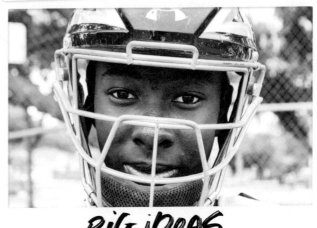

BIG IDEAS

ENTIRELY ABOUT THE SPIRIT OF PARTICIPATING IN ATHLETICS AT A YOUNG AGE,

THE "SHE PLAYS WE WIN" PROJECT CAN EXTEND TO ALL YOUNG WOMEN,

These girls are TALENTED,

FEARLESS,

FOR THE

Future!

NO MATTER WHAT SPORT THEY PLAY,
WHERE THEY'RE GROWING UP,

OR WHAT THEIR CIRCUMSTANCES ENTAIL.
-CHRISTIN ROSE, PHOTOGRAPHER

OUTLAWS
SOFTBALL

She Plays We Win is a photo campaign celebrating the confidence that sports provide young girls!

I HOPE ALL LADIES, AGE ZERO TO 100 YEARS YOUNG, CAN SEE A LITTLE PIECE OF THEMSELVES IN THIS BOOK. I HOPE YOU SEE THE CONFIDENCE IN THESE GIRLS' EYES . . . AND THAT YOU LEAVE KNOWING HOW MUCH CONFIDENCE AT THIS AGE IS A FOUNDATION FOR STRENGTH AND PERSEVERANCE FOR THE REST OF THEIR LIVES.

THIS BOOK IS DEDICATED to THESE GIRLS AND THE FEARLESS, DRIVEN WOMEN THEY WILL BECOME.

Dear Future Young Female Athletes,

You can do ANYTHING you want if you WORK HARD and PUT YOUR MIND to it. Playing sports is EMPOWERING. It has a way of making you want to be BETTER at everything you do in life, whether it be on the court, on the track, or in the classroom. There will be roadblocks and challenges along the way, but <u>NEVER GIVE UP</u> if it is something you LOVE.

ALWAYS BELIEVE in yourself and your DREAMS and ALWAYS GIVE your BEST. Remember to be HUMBLE and be PATIENT. Being GREAT at anything takes TIME and since GIRLS are the FUTURE, WE need to LIVE up to the fact that, <u>when we PLAY and give our best, we WIN, not only in sports but in LIFE!</u> Last, but not least, HAVE FUN! Enjoy the PROCESS and remember to be a RESPECTFUL competitor.

Wishing you ALL THE BEST!

Love,
Maya Rush

MAYA RUSH

"WHEN I RUN IN A RACE, I LIKE to THINK OF ALL THE PEOPLE WHO MAKE ME HAPPY IN LIFE. MY DESIRE TO MAKE THEM PROUD MOTIVATES ME to RUN FASTER."

BASKETBALL

"Basketball has taught me how to be a leader. It also teaches me how to work as a team and to always work hard."

VANESSA DE JESUS

JORDAN ALLEN

VANESSA DE JESUS

TATIANA GONZALEZ

KUMI TAMURA

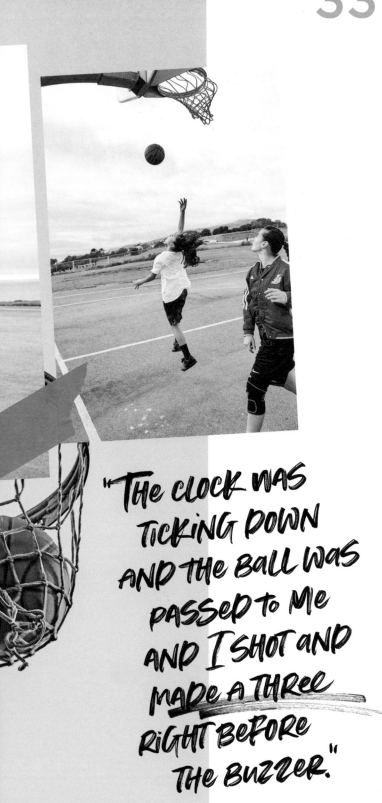

"THE CLOCK WAS TICKING DOWN AND THE BALL WAS PASSED TO ME AND I SHOT AND MADE A THREE RIGHT BEFORE THE BUZZER."

My Basketball Moment

KUMI TAMURA

There is that moment at the end of almost every basketball movie where the clock is winding down, the team is down by a point or two, everything is in slow motion, and you can hear the crowd suddenly go quiet with breathless anticipation. The point guard passes the ball, the shot goes up in super slow motion, and no one blinks or breathes, all eyes track the ball as it swishes through the net. The entire stadium erupts in cheers and applause. Freeze frame and the credits roll. I live for those moments. It's why I play the game.

My first eighth grade middle school game was crazy. We played against a school called Brentwood. They weren't that good, but since it was our team's first game together, it took some time to get into the flow and play as a team. We had the lead for most of the game but we let them come back, and Brentwood took the lead with just a few minutes left.

Luckily, we were able to tie the game and go into overtime. Then the second overtime! At the end of the second overtime, they scored a basket, they got fouled, and their player missed and then made a free throw. They were up by three with seconds to play. The clock was ticking down and the ball was passed to me and I shot and made a three right before the buzzer. The crown roared! It was the best feeling! I live for those moments.

The game was tied again and now, the third overtime was sudden death. The first score wins the game. Nobody scored for a while in the third overtime. My teammate and I decided to draw a foul to get to the free throw line. I tried but didn't get the call from the referee. My teammate did get a foul and stepped to the line to shoot a free throw for the win. The first shot rimmed out. I could tell she was nervous. The second shot went in and the game was over! We had won our first game together by one point in triple overtime! Now that was exciting!

"When I'm skateboarding, I can be me and I'm also FREE and nobody can stop me."

SKY BROWN

Lyla

LYLA KELLER
TRACK

Lyla feels awesome **"when someone is beating me or side-by-side and I'm able to push myself as hard as I can to try to win or tie."** Go Lyla!!

"It makes me feel proud of myself that I can do things I didn't think I could do and it makes me push myself even harder!"

Who is your role model? What do you want to be when you grow up?
"I have a lot of role models but Allyson Felix is my FAVORITE! She is kind, a super hard worker, and an amazing athlete!! I want to be a model and Olympic athlete first, then after that . . . Maybe a lawyer."

What are the top three things you need to have/do to succeed in your sport?

Focus, Determination, + Hard Work!

THIS RIGHT HERE
IS WHAT IT'S all ABOUT.

#ShePlaysWeWin ♡

"To Be A GOALKEEPER, you Gotta Be ToUGH. To Be a GOALkeeper, you Gotta Be FEARLESS."

CHARLOTTE MURRAY
SOCCER

CHARLOTTE

ZOE BENEDETTO
SURFER/SKATER

Z
O
E

"I LOVE THAT I AM ALWAYS SO HAPPY WHEN I SURF. I FEEL ENERGIZED AND RECHARGED WITH POSITIVITY!"

ViaNez

Nobody can stop Me!

SHE
PLAYS
WE WIN

TRACK*STARS*

360
CAB

CLOVER
CABELLERO

"NEVER GIVE UP,
NO MATTER IF YOU FALL,
GET UP AND KEEP GOING!"

VIANEZ MORALES
SKATER

California Dreaming

"IT'S ABOUT DOING WHAT YOU LOVE!"

KYRA WILLIAMS
SKATER

AHRIANA MARTINEZ

CARLY LONGO

MARISSA GORDON

ABYGIL CASTRO

ALONDRA DOMINGUEZ

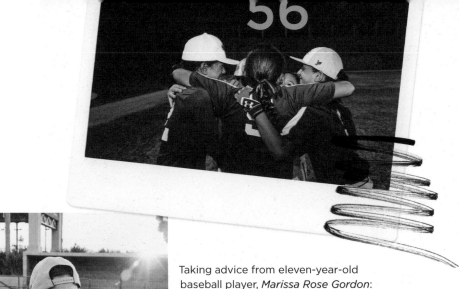

Taking advice from eleven-year-old baseball player, *Marissa Rose Gordon*: What advice would you give your five-year-old self?

"WHENEVER YOU FEEL LIKE YOU CAN'T GO ANYMORE, YOU HAVE TO PUSH THROUGH. WORKING HARD GETS YOU FAR IN LIFE."

MARISSA GORDON
BASEBALL

"I LOVE BASEBALL BECAUSE IT MAKES ME REALIZE GIRLS CAN DO ANYTHING BOYS CAN DO AND I ALSO JUST LOVE PLAYING THE SPORT.
I ALSO LIKE IT BECAUSE IT MAKES ME VERY HAPPY."

CARLY LONGO
BASEBALL

CHA RLI

CHARLI DEVRIES
HOCKEY

Charli now plays with girls, but at ten years old, she was the only girl on her ice hockey team and dealt with boys telling her she shouldn't be there many times. Her response:

"You can't get discouraged. No matter what anybody says to you, if you're good enough, you deserve to be there"

What advice would you give your five-year-old self?

"I'd tell myself to appreciate being in the moment. I would tell myself to give my everything all the time.

"It would be so cool if other girls that wanted to play ice hockey saw these photos, they will see me in all my gear and realize that it's not impossible and they can do it too.

"I love playing hockey because I love proving people wrong. I prove them wrong while doing what I love."

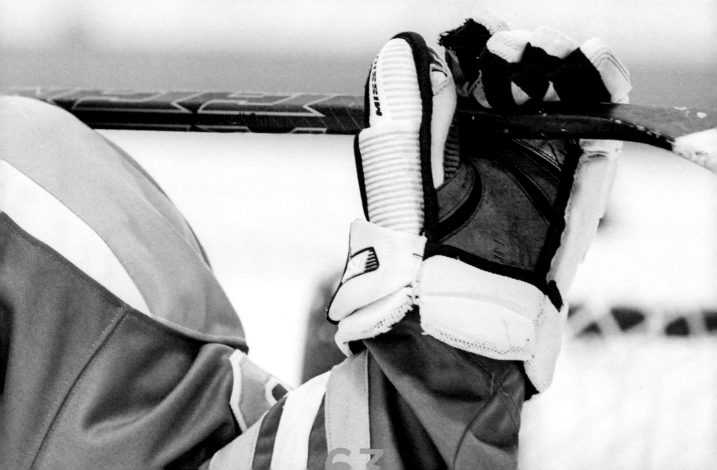

"If you're good enough,
you deserve to be there."
- Charli DeVries

Isabella

She Shot Her First Hole-in-one at 9 Years Old!

ISABELLA CUDA
GOLF

When asked if there's anything she can't do, Isabella replied:

"I was born with spina bifida and a tethered spinal cord. Doctors didn't think I would ever walk, but after undergoing two major spinal cord surgeries, I can walk, dance, swim, and golf like any other kid. I have no restrictions, so no, there is nothing I can't do!!!

"I like the combination of eye and hand coordination, strength, and tradition in golf. It is very relaxing but also challenging at the same time. And golf is a sport I can play my whole life."

67

Poppy Starr Olsen is an Australian Professional Skateboarder

67

POPPY
STARR
OLSEN

SKATEBOARDER

⊛ **NEWCASTLE,
AUSTRALIA**

"I'M ALL ABOUT
ENCOURAGING MORE
GIRLS TO SKATE!"

Barrel
Racing

SKYLAR ALVES
RODEO

"I LOVE BARREL RACING BECAUSE OF THE EXCITEMENT, THE FUN, THE SPEED, AND THE BUTTERFLIES I GET IN MY STOMACH WHEN I GO TO MAKE A RUN!"

GRACIE PEREZ
RODEO

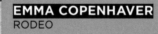

EMMA COPENHAVER
RODEO

"I have been riding since I was a baby with my mom in a baby backpack. My events are barrel racing, pole bending, goat tying, breakaway roping, and ribbon roping. I won my first saddle when I was six, running barrels."

KALI

"Tennis is a great sport. It teaches you self-confidence and helps you grow as a person, because you're out there by yourself for every point . . .

aND WHEN YOU'RE PLAYING, YOU HAVE TO BE YOUR OWN COACH, CHEERLEADER, aND MOTIVATOR."

KALLI MINOR
TENNIS

Hailie
Deegan

"*JUST A GIRL IN THE RACING WORLD WITH ONE GOAL IN MIND!*"

HAILIE DEEGAN

81

HAILIE DEEGAN

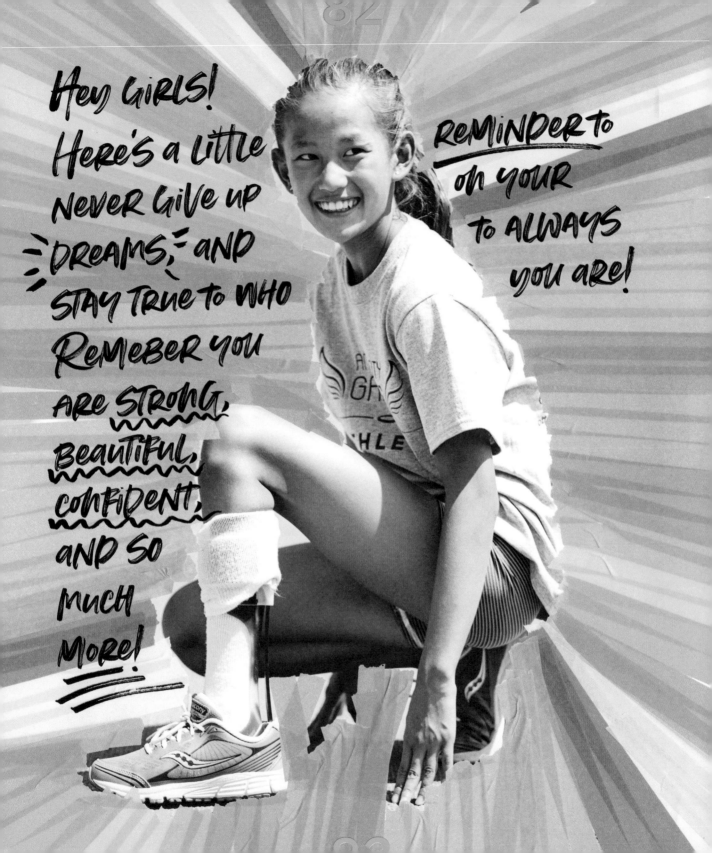

You're here to SHINE so don't be afraid to show the world who you are! Always BELIEVE in yourself and never doubt what you can and cannot do! You are UNSTOPPABLE, so don't let anyone get in the way of your dreams!! Most importantly, never forget to LOVE Yourself! You are WORTH SO MUCH!!

♡ ANNIE

ANNIE CAREY
TRACK

"I was adopted from China when I was almost two years old, and I had a clubfoot when I was born. After my parents brought me home and fixed my foot, I still had problems with my foot working, so I have to wear a brace so it will move up and down. When I was seven, I saw Oscar Pistorius run in the London Olympics and I told my mom I wanted to run in the Olympics and win a gold. After bugging her for a month, she found a paralympic club through the YMCA."

In 2019, Annie broke the world record and the Americas Record, for her disability, in the long jump at the Desert Challenge Games, and the Americas Record for high jump at Angel City Games. In addition, she was named to the US Junior Paralympic Track & Field Team and traveled to Nottwil, Switzerland, for the Junior World Championships, where she competed in the 100 meters, 200 meters, and long jump. At this competition she set a personal record in the 100 meters and received the bronze medal. In the 200 meters she beat her personal record and broke the Americas Record.

Annie was then named to the US Paralympic Track & Field Team for the Parapan American Games, where she competed in Lima, Peru, in the 100 meters and the long jump, receiving the bronze medal for the United States in both events!

NORA MANGER
DOWNHILL
LONGBOARDER

"You will find people who will support you in skating, NO matter what, and who will help you along the way."

What are the top three qualities you
have to have to succeed in your sport?

Tough, Brave,

& WILLING to GET SOME SCRAPES.

How do you feel when you accomplish something you never have before on a longboard?

"Excited. Exhilarated. Accomplished. Wild. Free. I'm always really happy when I do something new because sometimes it is a lot of pain getting there. But, it is always another small step in making me a better skater."

What advice would you give to your five-year-old self?

"Don't put that tennis ball in the toilet. Nothing good will come of it! Haha! No, really, I'd tell myself to not worry whether my toys are blue or pink. Just go for the toys and activities that speak to you. Have fun. And, don't try to grow up too quickly. You'll have the whole rest of your life to be an adult."

Anything else you want to tell us about downhill longboarding that we might not know?

"Maryhill is often called the Mecca for downhill. It's a curvy, 2.2-mile-long closed road in Washington state. Riding there has changed my life. I've been skating for two years. But I've only really been doing downhill longboarding for about a year. I used to kick around my neighborhood and do some small hills. But I had never even considered bombing down a big hill until I got to Maryhill and met so many rad and supportive people. I'm now a member of the Maryhill Ratz Longboarding Team. The Maryhill Ratz are a family of fun-loving downhill fanatics who are happy to practice a lot, teach others, and share their love of the sport."

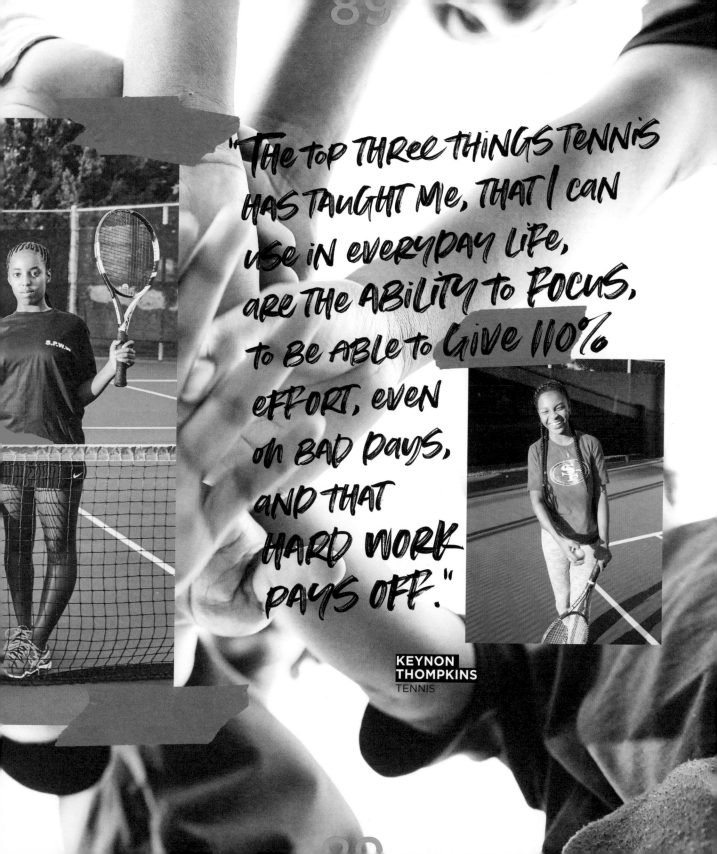

"The top three things tennis has taught me, that I can use in everyday life, are the ability to focus, to be able to give 110% effort, even on bad days, and that HARD WORK PAYS OFF."

KEYNON THOMPKINS
TENNIS

BREANA COOK
TENNIS

KAMRYN + KAYLEE

KAYLEE WU
GOLFER FROM
MEDFORD, OR
(ROSE'S HOMETOWN!)

What are the top three things you
need to have to succeed in golf?

Determination. Patience. Focus!

"Determination is something you need for sure—if you want to get where you're going, it's a lot of reps, you're out here for hours and hours and hours. The golf course is like a second home, I've been out here since I was six—it's something that I will carry with me forever."

KAMRYN FORD
GOLF

SOFIA
+
Cailee

SOFIA QUINTERO

CAILEE LOLA

"Stay Strong + Work THROUGH it!"

SOFIA QUINTERO
SOFTBALL

"Softball teaches me how to be tough—there could be situations where you and your team are making a bunch of errors or you're really behind, but it teaches you to stay through the tough situations. You can face a bump in your life, but since I've experienced this through softball, I just know I have to stay strong and work through it!"

CAILEE LOLA
SOFTBALL

Cailee Lola on the importance of kindness:

"Some people might be more natural or better than you. You just have to remember it's not only how good they are at the sport—but it also matters their sportsmanship, how they act around other players, and if they're kind."

Be KIND!

#SHEPLAYSWEWIN

AKIRA

"To do Jiu Jitsu, you have to be committed, take risks, and not be afraid of losing. Because whenever you lose, you also LEARN."

AKIRA BUA
JIU JITSU

"When I accomplish something new in Jiu Jitsu, it makes me feel like I'm on top of the world. But I know these feelings are fleeting and the next day, even though I have a gold medal in hand, it's back to the drawing board. My dad says in his art, "You are only as good as your next painting." And that's how I feel about Jiu Jitsu. I am only as good as my next match.

"Jiu Jitsu is known as the gentle art, but what most people don't know is that it is also the art of strangulation and putting someone to sleep. But I like the idea that it's just pure art."

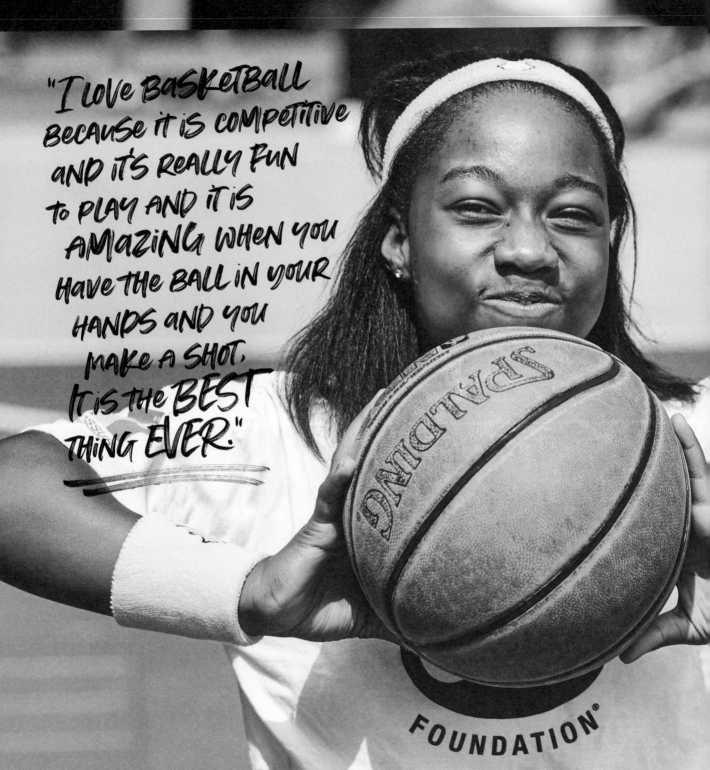

"I LOVE BASKETBALL BECAUSE IT IS COMPETITIVE AND IT'S REALLY FUN TO PLAY AND IT IS AMAZING WHEN YOU HAVE THE BALL IN YOUR HANDS AND YOU MAKE A SHOT, IT IS THE BEST THING EVER."

SHANAYHA
WELSH
BASKETBALL

FOR THE JOY & LOVE OF THE GAME, THIS IS

SHE
PLAYS
WE WIN

SADIE HUIZENGA
GYMNAST

To the girls chasing
their dreams every day,
#ShePlaysWeWin

ONLY AFTER SHE LOST HER WINGS DID SHE LEARN the TRUE MEANING OF FLYING!

LILLY BIAGINI
MULTI-SPORT ATHLETE

I am Lilly! THIS iS MY STORY...

I was born with a rare disorder called "arthrogryposis multiplex congenita"—WHAT? Hang on, I'll explain!

Twisted and contorted I came screaming into life. No one had ever seen a baby like me before. The first twenty-four hours was a roller coaster for my mom. "She will never swallow, she is blind, she is deaf, she will never move, she is cognitively impaired, and she may die within the next twenty-four hours!"

This was my mom's first conversation after awakening from the C-section.

However, my mom had faith. And with her faith and her endless strength, I was only affected from the mid-thigh down. I did not have kneecaps, and most of the bones in my feet were missing or in the wrong place. My muscles were very tight and I could not bend . . . at all!

My legs looked like they were on backward, and the banding was isolated only my lower extremities.

From one month old to six years old, I was in and out of surgeries and casts. However, throughout all this my spirit and confidence were growing rapidly. I was never given the option to give up or stop exploring playgrounds or the simplest things as if they were a toy store.

I have to say, it was hard—very, very hard—to accept that I was never going to walk. Well, if I can be honest,

it was mostly hard on my mom. I spent countless hours crying with her. But the bottom line is, I am healthy and happy. I just can't walk.

I know, I know, easy to say now, and easier yet to say when I am not your child. Truth is, there are situations much more difficult and tragic than mine, and we will survive and thrive, no matter what! And that is the attitude I have to have to get through!!

Now let's get to the most extraordinary life-changing moment. Are you still comfortable? If not, get cozy and let me tell you, this moment will forever change the way you look at life.

Remember I am healthy, sweet and smart, sassy and ever challenging. Just like I should be, just like I always have been, and I can breathe again. Is this anticipation killing you? Well hold on, I promise I'll tell you.

It was January 2014. I was with my mom at a typical checkup appointment. As my mom had to leave the room for a moment, I took this opportunity to show my surgeon something I had been working on: walking on my knees! This was something that seemed impossible to everyone but me. I raced down the hallway like something was chasing me, and when I turned around, doctors, my mom, and many others' mouths were wide open and it was silent.

WHAT THE HECK!

Well, it TURNS out I am, AND will always be, one in a million!

That whole "walking on her knees" thing was a new development that my doctors found very interesting, and I was quickly taken in to have new Xrays done.

OK, wait a minute, what's going on?!

Well, turned out that my scoliosis, torticollis, and kyphosis had become "functional." But most importantly, I proved that my muscular/skeletal system could bear my own weight. By developing my own funny little way of walking on my knees, I proved that I could hold myself up and that my legs rotated in the hip sockets correctly.

OMG. This whole time, no one realized that what I was doing was getting myself ready to walk—really walk. I'll never forget when the doctor said: "We were just waiting for Lilly to show us what she could do!" My response was, "I want to walk."

But in order to achieve that, they said I would have to have both legs amputated at the knee.

Wow, you want to talk about choices! God bless my mom. Try making that choice for your six-year-old daughter.

It was a long ride home that day. Long and very quiet. Our world (weird as it was) had just taken an enormously different and new direction.

Don't misunderstand me, my mom has been making impossible decisions for me from the time I was born . . . but really . . .

My feet hurt more often, they were cold most of the time, and I was well aware that they didn't work. I know that my mom and I were facing a serious surgery and big changes, but my mom was very pragmatic about it all. Believe it or not, my only questions were "Where do my legs go when the doctors take them, and will they grow back?" "Will my new legs have toes that we can paint—and can I walk?" We talk about it every day, and with each question came more realization that life was about to change again—for the better!

Strange, funny little things helped put it into perspective for me, like when my mom took the bottom parts of a Barbie doll's legs off and showed me how it would look. Shriners gave me a teddy bear who had had an amputation. We read books on amputation and talked to a child psychologist, all in preparation. Honestly, I think what helped the most was my mom repeatedly telling me that regardless of what we did, I would always be fabulous. I'm smart, witty, and strong willed. Regardless of what legs are and can

or cannot do, I will be just fine, and I'm loved with or without limits!

Have I lost your attention yet? Are you still on this journey with me? Great, because my life-changing day happened on February 13, 2014! Whooo! Excited but terrified.

HAVE YOU EVER FELT LIKE SINGING OUT LOUD, DANCING THROUGH THE HOUSE WITH COMPLETE ABANDON, AND REJOICING OVER EVERY MOMENT OF EVERY DAY?

Well, that's sort of the way I was feeling! My mom felt like she hadn't been able to adequately describe what this journey has really been like, but today, finally, both she and I feel free again!

And now I am sure you are wondering, "Where and what am I doing now?"

Well, I am twelve years old now and live in Texas . . .

I am still unstoppable and fabulous!

My legs have been to seven different states, horseback riding, golfing, snowboarding, running, and of course, I've gotten a few pedicures!

Lilly you are an inspiration to us all. With this attitude and spirit, you will always be unstoppable! Keep pushing forward every day and you will go SO far!

xoxo, Christin Rose

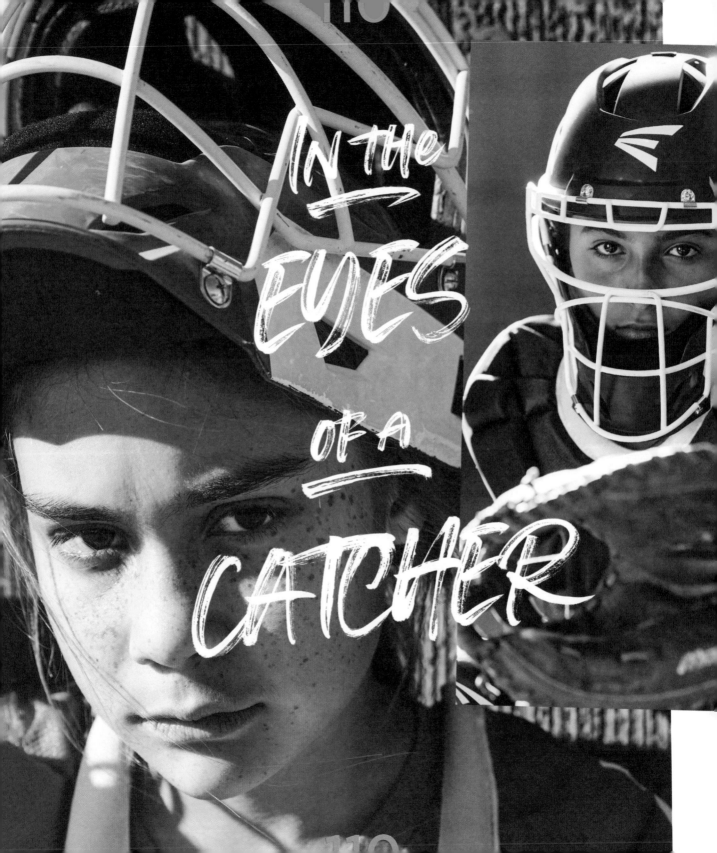

IN THE EYES OF A CATCHER

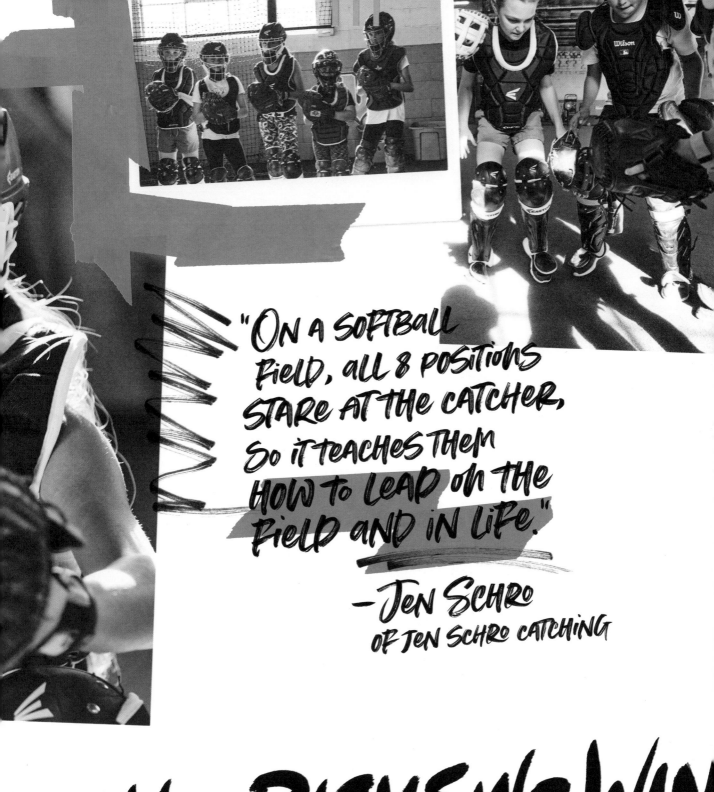

"ON A SOFTBALL FIELD, ALL 8 POSITIONS STARE AT THE CATCHER, SO IT TEACHES THEM HOW TO LEAD ON THE FIELD AND IN LIFE."

—JEN SCHRO
OF JEN SCHRO CATCHING

#SHEPLAYSWEWIN

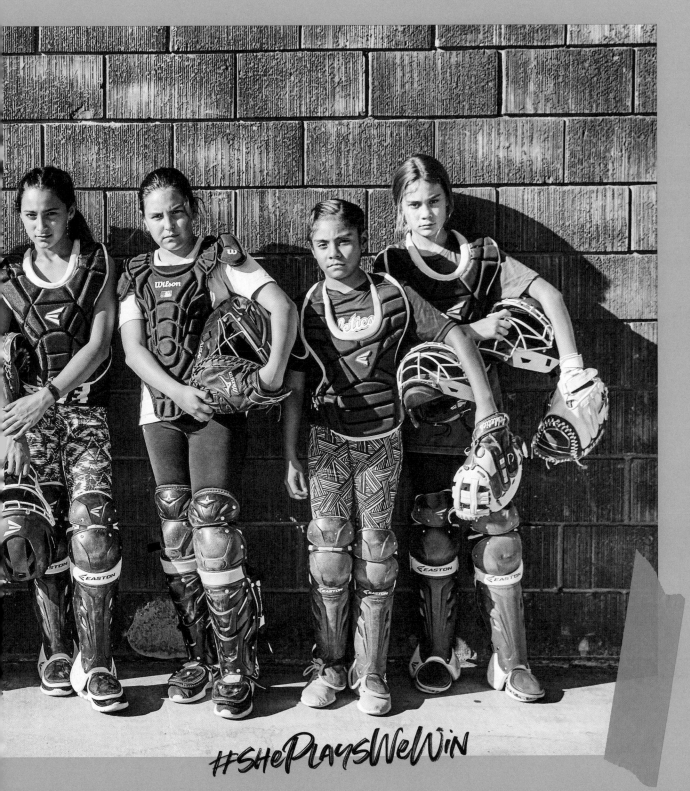

#ShePlaysWeWin

"I WANT PEOPLE TO KNOW NOT ONLY HOW HARD SOFTBALL PLAYERS WORK, BUT HOW MUCH OF A DIFFERENCE SPORTS MAKE IN OTHER WOMEN'S LIVES."
— DEVYN DELANEY

DEVYN DELANEY
CATCHER

119

#ShePlaysWeWin

"BUT NEVER QUIT!"

**BROOKLYN
SKYE JONES**
BOXER

LET'S ROLL!

QUINNE DANIELS
JORDYN BARRATT
SKY BROWN

SKATE Like a GiRL!

MINNA STESS
SKY BROWN
QUINNE DANIELS

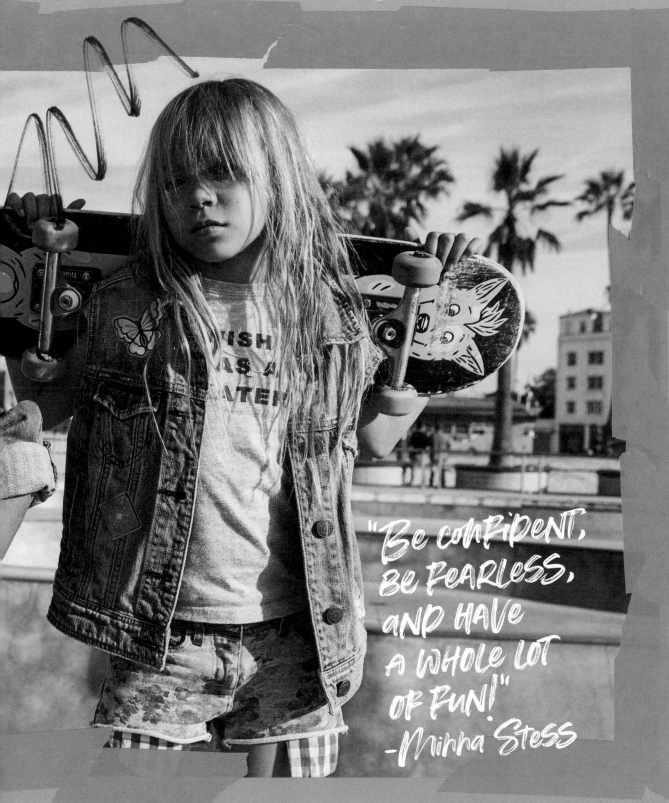

"Be confident, be fearless, and have a whole lot of fun!"
-Minna Stess

SHOT IN COLLABORATION WITH

OPENING ceremony in New York, NY

"WHEN we FALL DOWN, we GeT RiGHT BaCK uP."

MAYA BRYSON
KALEA BROWN
RACHEL GLENN
MAYA RUSH

"THE THING I LOVE MOST ABOUT MY TRACK TEAM IS THAT WE ALWAYS JOKE AROUND, BUT WHEN IT'S TIME TO COMPETE, WE PUT OUR GAME FACES ON AND WE GO HARD OR WE GO HOME."

RACHEL GLENN
TRACK & FIELD

THESE GIRLS Fly!

SYDNEY KENNETT
INDOOR SKYDIVER

RYAN KENNETT
MOTOCROSS

AUDREY SHIN
FIGURE SKATER

"MY FAVORITE STYLE OF CLIMBING IS BOULDERING BECAUSE OF THE OVERHUNG WALLS AND VERY POWERFUL, DYNAMIC MOVES."

ALINA ALBERT
ROCK CLIMBING

Alina Albert is twelve years old and one of the top youth female rock climbers in the country.

Alina has earned a spot on Team USA for the past six seasons, and has consistently finished top three in every local and regional competition for the past four years, including competitions open to collegiate and adult athletes.

She's currently training at Mesa Rim on their competitive team and has her eyes set to compete in the 2022 Youth Summer Olympics and the 2024 Summer Olympics.

"The reason I like climbing is because it involves both mental and physical strength. I like the challenge of having to use both of these skills."

I HOPE THESE PHOTOS INSPIRE YOU ... YOUR DAUGHTER, YOUR MOTHER, YOUR SISTER ... EVEN IF ONE PHOTO SPEAKS + TAKES YOU BACK TO THE FIELD— IF YOU SEE YOURSELF OR SOMEONE YOU LOVE IN THE EYES OF THESE IMAGES, THEN MY MISSION IS COMPLETE.

—CHRISTIN ROSE

LONDON & TEAGAN MEZA
WITH THEIR MOM, ANDIE MEZA

SHe PLAYS we WIN

ALL GIRLS BASEBALL

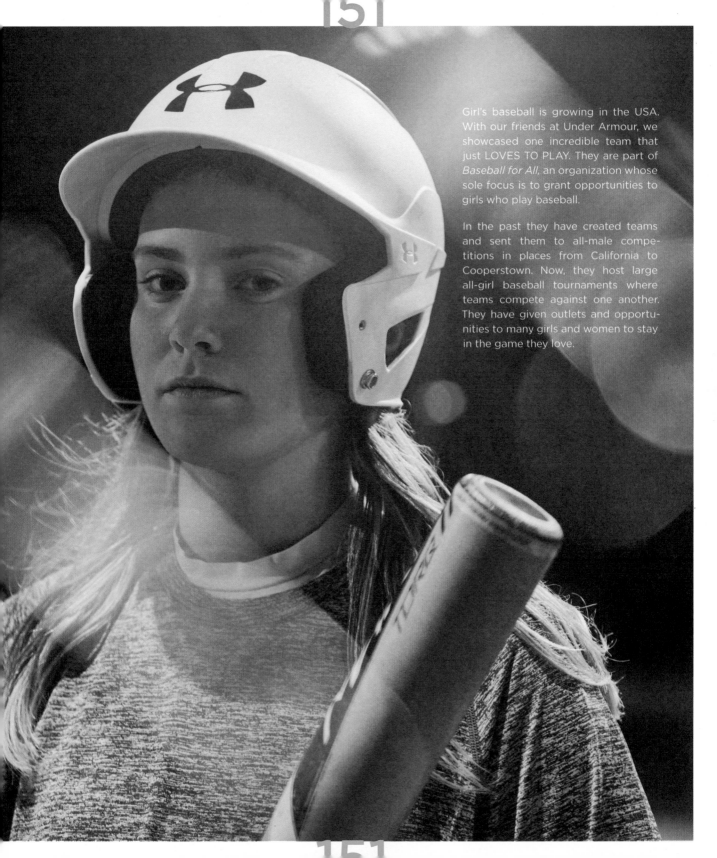

Girl's baseball is growing in the USA. With our friends at Under Armour, we showcased one incredible team that just LOVES TO PLAY. They are part of *Baseball for All*, an organization whose sole focus is to grant opportunities to girls who play baseball.

In the past they have created teams and sent them to all-male competitions in places from California to Cooperstown. Now, they host large all-girl baseball tournaments where teams compete against one another. They have given outlets and opportunities to many girls and women to stay in the game they love.

PALOMA BENACH

"These girls are my sisters. We live far from one another, we all deal with different crap, but when we're together, it's like nothing else matters. We forget our problems, we play ball the way we know how. And no matter what, we have each other's backs. Through thick and thin, we are always there for each other. And no matter what we might be going through, we never bring it onto the field. Because that's where we play."

BRITTANY APGAR

"I was born without my right hand. The doctors weren't completely sure why my hand never formed but they said I punched my hand out of my mom's womb so it never fully developed. It's a condition known as hypoplasia—a decrease in blood cells in major organs or arteries.

"Since I've never had a hand I've never known any different, so I never knew what people meant when they called me an inspiration because I just did what I could and learned how to do stuff I couldn't. I've never really had a problem with bullies or anything. But I have had a problem with people not respecting me . . . That quickly changes when I show them who I am as a person—that my disability does not define my character.

"This shoot was one of the most important moments in my life. It finally gives me a chance to impact people on a larger scale than what I'm capable of. I think it's important for people to hear my story to raise awareness that no matter who you are or where you come from, you can make a change in the world. Things will get better, you just have to see it out.

"No matter what you do or what you want—you can do it. Even if there are people that give you hate. Someone's got to be strong enough to make the change and pave the path for other people."

"MY DISABILITY DOES NOT DEFINE MY CHARACTER."
-BRITTANY APGAR

BRITTANY APGAR
BASEBALL

Zapper

Speedy Wonder

Poison Ivy

LA Junior DERBY

Mojo   Bella Blitz   Sweet Baby Rage

DOLLS

"IF YOU FALL DOWN, YOU GET BACK UP, YOU JUST KEEP TRYING UNTIL YOU ACHE SO MUCH YOU CAN'T TRY AGAIN. THEN YOU TRY AGAIN THE NEXT DAY..."
-TINY TERROR

Be yourself and

Be PART OF SOMETHING!

I had the privilege of photographing the incredible girls of the *LA Junior Derby Dolls*. They are the junior program associated with the *LA Derby Dolls*, Southern California's premier all-female, banked track roller derby league. Many of the girls' moms are into roller derby, passing the toughness and grit down through the generations.

The overarching themes for these girls are independence, strength, and confidence. And as twelve-year-old Speedy Wonder simply states, "Derby is Life." After spending the day with these girls in their East LA training warehouse, I can confirm, that's exactly how they all feel. They are dedicated to each other and to the competitiveness of derby. It's teaching them to be unique, to be themselves, to be a part of something, and of course that when they fall down to get right back up . . . something they will use forever.

Ten-year-old Tiny Terror explains, "I love the lesson roller derby teaches us. If you fall down you get back up, you just keep trying until you ache so much you can't try again. And then you try again the next day. Once you get it you move on to the next thing. It is a repetitive pattern that keeps your adrenaline going and makes you want to do more of it. Also, when you have a teammate, they are not just a teammate, they become a friend."

"I really got into playing once I met all the other girls. I didn't want to play a sport with other people if the other people wouldn't support me. But they all did. **I felt like I had really met my people—my big, fat, skating family.**" —Mojo, twelve years old

"Derby is LiFE"

-Speedy Wonder

Ya Gotta Have HEART

ZAILA AVANT-GARDE
BASKETBALL

As part of the SPWW partnership with Under Armour, we made a trip to New Orleans and met a hooper bursting with HEART with a lot of tricks up her sleeve. This is Zaila!

"I would tell my four-year-old self to keep working and to have BIG dreams. When I was little I never thought that I'd ever be as good as I am at basketball so soon. But now I know if I just keep practicing I can do almost anything."

DREAM BIG.

HUSTLE HARD.

Zaila

"My DREAM is to one DAY Be THE BEST WNBA PLAYER EVER."

Avant-Garde

LOS ANGELES
JETS
TRACK CLUB

"You have to run and gotta run fast—You're not trying to beat each other, you're trying to beat yourself!"
—Chloe Hayden

The *LA Jets Track Club* team has grown to be 185 athletes since its founding in 1973. With 202 Individual National Champions, 156 National Championship Relay Teams, and 66 National Records, this group has earned their place in the spotlight. They believe in creating a community that encourages their athletes to excel in athletics, academics, and moral excellence. SHE PLAYS WE WIN features a group of these young girls and gets a glimpse into what they describe as their track family.

SHe PLAYS WeWIN

"THe GiRLS on My TEAM ARe My SISTERS."

-Spencer YOUNG

#SHePLAYSWeWIN

"TRACK TEACHES ME
TO BE A LEADER
BECAUSE IT GAVE ME
THE STRENGTH AND A
STRONG MIND TO
DO THE RIGHT THING.
I HAVE LEARNED TO
BE CONFIDENT, AND IT
TAUGHT ME TO STAND UP
AND STAND OUT."
—Spencer Young

♡
FAMILY

JUST RUN YOUR RACE!

ZARA PERCY
SKATER

"Sometimes when I'm skating, I just feel free, like I'm flying away on my skateboard."

With girls skateboarding on a steady rise across the country, SPWW decided to spend a day at the skate park with five girls pursuing the sport. Unanimously they tell me the coolest part of skating is all the other girls they meet along the way. There's an overall attitude of encouragement among the girls and a belief that if you fall down you HAVE to keep trying and get back up again. An attitude of perseverance shines through these girls, and they welcome any girls who want to join them to try skateboarding!

SKATE

"BOXING MAKES
ME FEEL POWERFUL,
LIKE I CAN DO
ANYTHING."
- Jaxon Bowes

JAXON
BOWES

BOXER

⊛ **LOS ANGELES, CA**

Jaxon Bowes was born in Downtown Los Angeles in 2012. She began training and developed a passion for boxing at only three and a half years old.

Jaxon's goal is to join the 2028 Olympic Games and win a gold medal. More importantly, she wants to be a role model to kids all over the world and show them boxing is not only about fighting but also about developing confidence and discipline.

She is now six and a half years old and she is showing everyone that you can build the strength and courage to stand up for yourself, regardless of age and gender.

LONDON GOLAS
SOCCER

"When I'm on the Field, I'm only Focused on the Game."

"I have loved soccer ever since I was old enough to do it. As I grow as a player, some things have made it even more fun than it already was. One of the things is playing with people that I know and am friends with. Over this school year I was able to play soccer for my school alongside my friends. This was one of the best experiences I have had. Also just tuning in and only thinking about the game made it so much better.

"One last thing makes sports in general so much more fun for me. It's trying things I wouldn't normally do. The thrill of doing something I didn't know I could do on the pitch is amazing! My advice to any girl out there wanting to get into sports is just to try new things. This past spring I tried a new thing which has changed me as an athlete. I tried a new sport, aka lacrosse. I suggest trying new things to everyone no matter what. If you wanna do it just go for it. I want all the girls reading this or anyone reading this to know one thing. That thing is <u>you are amazing, you are fearless, and YOU ARE YOU!</u>"

HUSTLE, HEART,

+ OUR FUTURE!

I HOPE THIS BOOK KEEPS MOMENTUM GOING FOR WHAT THE GREAT WOMEN BEFORE US HAVE STARTED. I HOPE, NO MATTER IF ROBOTS RULE THE WORLD, WE AS A SOCIETY CELEBRATE AND RECOGNIZE THE IMPORTANCE OF GIRLS PARTICIPATING IN SPORTS!

XOXO,

CHRISTIN ROSE

#SPWW

Ok- So as much as this book is about the girls on these pages, it is just as much about you! and our story is bigger than this book! So get some pens, tape, scissors, and pics. Let's write the rest of this story TOGETHER!

xoxo, CHRISTIN Rose

- ☐ Tape
- ☐ Pens
- ☐ Scissors
- ☐ + Pics

Let's DO THIS!

my name is

_____

but sometimes friends call me

_____

i've been alive for

_____ **yrs**   _____ **mos**   _____ **days**

i live and breathe

_____
(sport)

my biggest achievement (so far) was when i

_____

_____

_____

_____

(tape a pic . . . or three . . . of your
beautiful, fierce self here)

also . . .
make all this white paper
as vibrant as you feel!

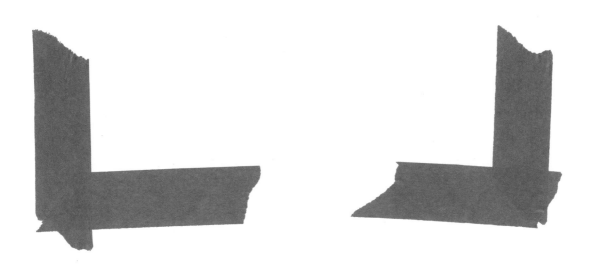

i am grateful for my ability to

---

three things my team/coach says about me

---

i will never stop

---

three things i want my future self to remember and hold close to my heart

---

---

to get even better i promise myself i will

---

in one year, my goal is to . . .

in five years, my goal is to . . .

to get there i will . . .

to get there i will . . .

now repeat after me. i am

_____

_____

and

_____

and i'm going to change the world when i

_____

_____

_____

_____

xo xo,

_____

THIS IS JUST THE BEGINNING.

"SKATING MAKES ME
FEEL ALIVE!"
-Kala Baltasar

THANK YOU

I HAVE LEARNED THINGS FROM THESE LITTLE GIRLS...♥

SHE PLAYS WE WIN has become so much more than a photo project to me. **This right here is my heart**.

I started this project to help contribute positive imagery to modern day media, but the truth is, this project ended up changing me as a person forever. Each and every one of these girls taught me more than I could ever imagine about **grit** and **guts** and **sisterhood**.

So, **thank you girls**! I'm constantly in awe of you and forever grateful.

I also want to thank everyone who believed in me, especially my friends at Under Armour, who shined a light on this project. Thanks to those who continue to believe in the importance of empowering young women in athletics. I'll never forget my time on the field, and I know that whenever we encourage girls to get

in the game, we're fostering in them all the beautiful lessons of **victory**, **defeat**, **discipline**, and **determination**.

And a very special thank you to my parents—Jim and Deb Palazzolo—for believing in me since day one. Without you, none of this would have been possible.

xoxo,
Christin Rose

I've been Reminded to stay SO True to myself and to Not be bothered by all the Noise we Deal with everyday in media & society. To Not let anything affect my confidence!
— Christin Rose

CHRISTIN ROSE
& QUINNE DANIELS

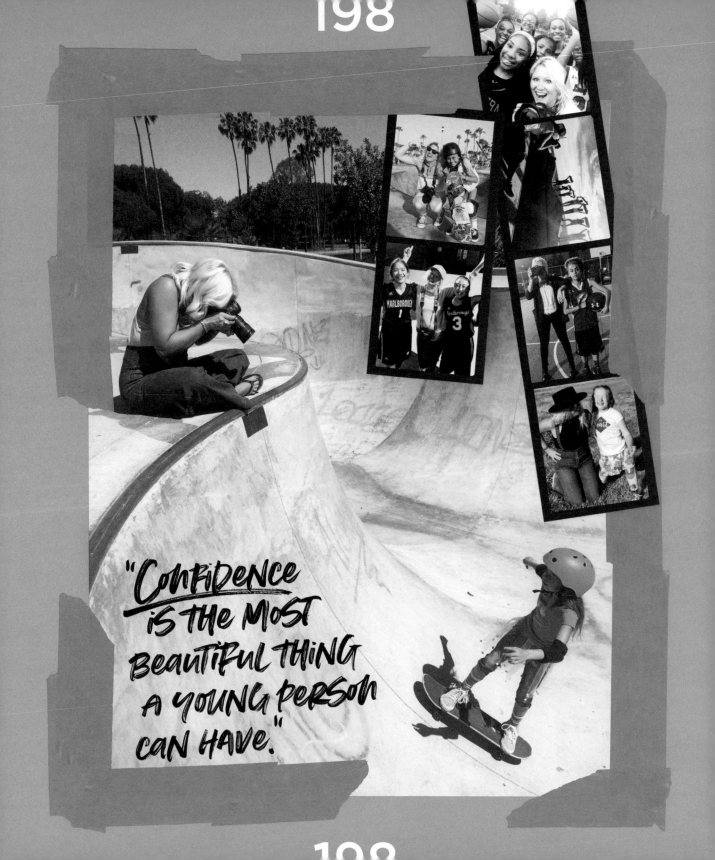

"CONFIDENCE IS THE MOST BEAUTIFUL THING A YOUNG PERSON CAN HAVE."

ABOUT CHRISTIN ROSE

Christin Rose lives to uplift people with her photography. Her upbeat and enthusiastic vibe drives her work. She looks at each opportunity to photograph someone as a chance to tell their story . . . to celebrate who they are.

Nearly four years ago, Rose started SHE PLAYS WE WIN—a project that would go on to spark a conversation about the positive effects athletics create for young women. Inspired by her own experiences in sports, this project is the heartbeat of her photography.

Empowering women and girls is a theme that is carried through all of her photography work. Rose loves Italian food and classic rock. She went to the University of Oregon and now lives in Austin, Texas, with her husband, River Jordan.

"It's so incredibly important to highlight these young women now before they get to an age when they question themselves. If we create more images like these, it will inevitably increase self-esteem for young women, and that's the ultimate goal!"

THOUGH THE PAGES OF OUR BOOK COME TO A CLOSE, OUR SUPPORT OF GIRLS CONTINUES ON!

We're so proud of our partnership with, and proceeds donation to, the Women's Sports Foundation. Their mission—to enable girls and women to reach their potential in sport and life—is something we believe in, whole heartedly. And everyone who purchases this book joins us in supporting, celebrating, and believing in the power of girls.

Women's Sports Foundation

The WSF is an ally, advocate, and catalyst. Founded by Billie Jean King in 1974, the Foundation strengthens and expands participation and leadership opportunities through its research, grants and fellowships, educational curricula, mentoring events, and wide range of community programs. WSF is a leading voice driving gender equity in sport and has positively shaped the lives of millions of youth, high school and collegiate student-athletes, elite athletes, and coaches. The Women's Sports Foundation is building a future where every girl and woman can #KeepPlaying. **All girls. All women. All sports.**

To learn more, please visit **WomensSportsFoundation.org**.

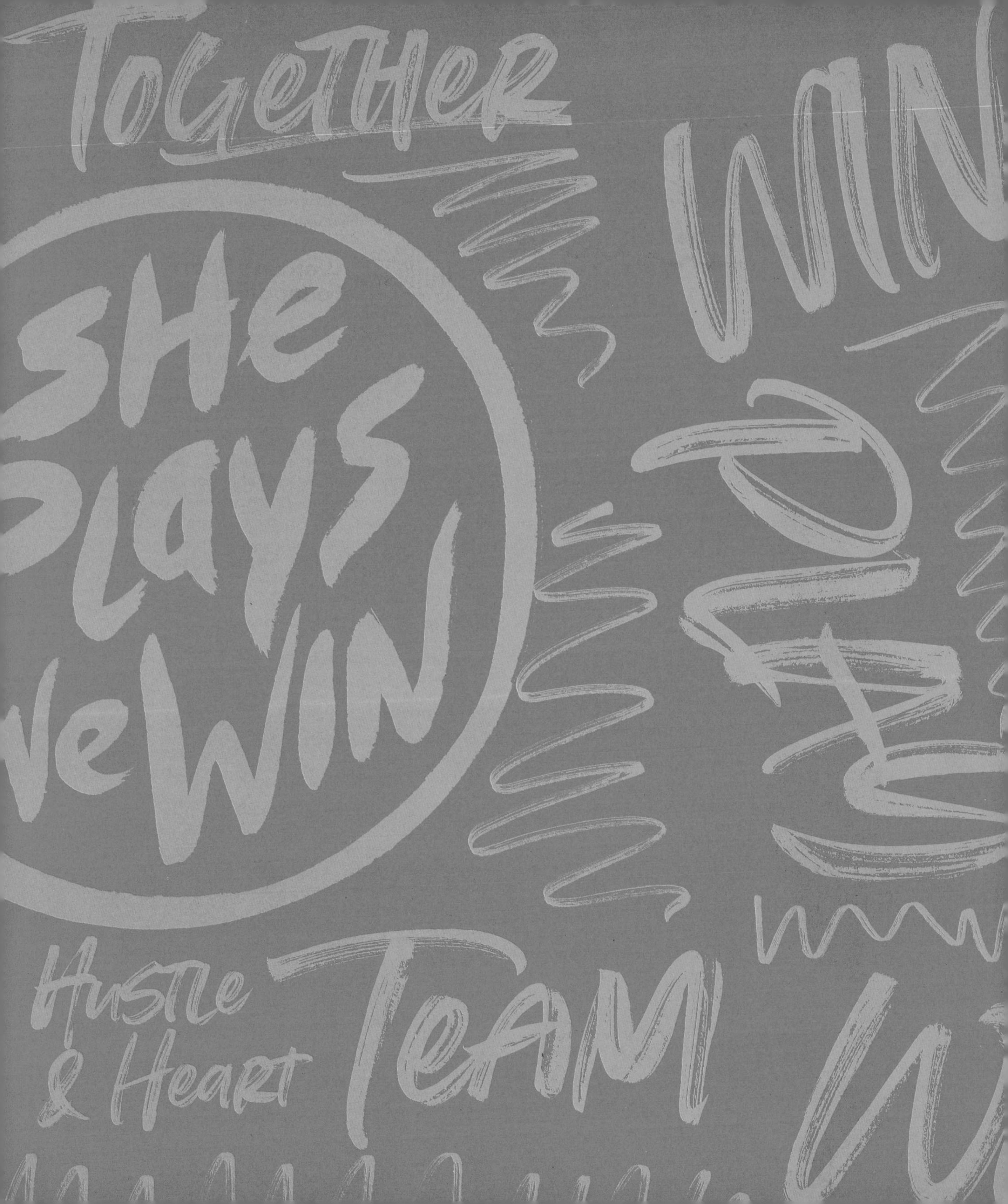
Together
SHE
WIN
Hustle & Heart
Team